Love, Sins and Heartbreak

Rachel Parker

BookLeaf Publishing

Presentation by *BookLeaf Publishing*

Web: www.bookleafpub.com

E-mail: info@bookleafpub.com

ISBN: 9789395026598

First edition 2022

DEDICATION

To anyone that buys this book,

I love you.

ACKNOWLEDGEMENT

No matter how many poems and drafts I had in the works, it is still so difficult to decide what the book should be about. So, I want to give thanks to my friends Shannon and Brianna, who helped me slow down my thoughts enough to actually create the concept of this book, and for their advice that pulled me out of the hole I was digging with my rambles. I appreciate you.

Jealous Eyes

I'm jealous of the way your eyes dance over
other people.

The way that they met hers under the light of the
setting sun.

The way that they wouldn't leave each others
until you'd met in the middle.

All while you missed the way that mine admired
you from by your side.

The way they cursed me with the memory of
how your eyes looked with laughter in them.

And haunted me with the sight of your eyes
meeting hers in a way they'd never met mine, the
look of love I'd always hoped to receive from
you.

I'm embarrassed that when you finally caught
my eyes that you caught them when I was
breaking.

Closing them in resignation hiding the tears that
were about to come,

I'd missed the eyes following my every move with their own sort of heartbreak in them.

The ones that were jealous that my eyes never stopped looking for yours even while you were looking at hers.

There's No Stopping Love

You can't stop someone from loving you

It's something that is never told.

They can preach that you can't love until you
love yourself

But if I may be so bold

I'm gonna love you, even when you don't.

And you'll think that the world should be
against you

And I'll tell you exactly why it won't.

We're not perfect you and I

But I can tell you that my passion for you will
never be a lie

I will never not want you in my life.

Made For Each Other

If we were slow dancing in a burning room,

Would you only think about our impending doom?

Or would you love me in our last moments as fierce as the fire burns around us,

As fierce as I have loved you since our start.

There must be something bone-deep in us telling us how we are made for each other.

For not even the end of our world could tear us apart.

From one world onto the next, I'll carry you with me.

So that we can make it ours again.

Tease

Let us rewrite our history

I'll start a new religion from the gasps you make
while I'm on my knees

Treating you as my favourite mystery

I promise to get you screaming out 'please'

To tease your wants from your lips

Is proving to be my greatest wish.

The Love You Crave

I crave the intimacy of falling asleep with a
smile on my face

Holding a lover's hand close to my chest

Hair whisping away under our slow breaths.

The idea of someone you care for being there
when you wake up

Greeting you with the same smile as when you
fell asleep

With sunlight caressing our skin

And no fear as to how we look

Is it any wonder that I crave silences like this?

Always so comfortable that we both fall into it

Gazes dancing across each other's faces,
dropping down our bodies in a bid to memorise
the moment.

The comfort of wearing too-big clothes in a person.

A feeling of self when you're with someone else.

Love & Life

I want to leave a stain on life

The same way that tea stains the page of your favourite book

Or the way that wine stubbornly clings to the fabric of your favourite dress

I want to stay there in a way that will say that I was here, that you won't forget me anytime soon

I want it to be found years later and for people to think about why a part of me was left

I want to be known

For people to imagine how I lived my life even while they are living theirs

I want to have a hold on something

As it's something I never quite got to do when I was here

I want my love to have somewhere to go despite
the fact that I won't

Unspoken

I love you, I do

I'm always half in love with you.

There's just something about you,

That I know could have led to something true.

If it wasn't for the way we met

I know I could have loved you more than you'd
ever know

I've always been half in love with you

But it's not something that I've ever said

We're not playing a game here

Especially after all that's happened

But we are playing second fiddle to the
unwritten rules

That are all that's keeping this from its inevitable
end

I don't know how not to love at least some part
of you,

But I do know that there was something
unspoken there.

Lust

Wandering hands, sly smiles, loving in the dark.

Restless resting, tossing sheets, dreams that
haunt you on nights you can't sleep.

Zips undone, buttons popped, impatience means
they aren't going anywhere fast.

It's bodies moving bodies, an orchestra of sound
teased from a person and subconscious
movement you hope others never see.

Hands fisted in hair otherwise matted,

Breathless gasps against glistening skin.

"Mine" they whisper and "Yours" you promise.

A dance of dominance and submission reaching
a climax, a satisfied completion.

Gluttony

You indulge by habit, saying yes when you
wonder if now is when they'll begin to hate you.

You've never said no to an offer before, why
start now?

It's not a competition, more of a temptation.

You always want what isn't yours to have and at
this point, your friends think is a thing that you
lack.

Happy to be the other woman, to take all that
you can.

You don't see a reason to stop, it never crossed
your mind that you wouldn't stay on top.

On top of a world of your own creation, always
throwing yourself into situations that will garner
attention.

Thinking yourself to be flawless when in reality
you make yourself the villain at every turn-

You never know when to stop giving in to your little fantasy, where nothing is a concern.

Pride

Drowning under all the words you couldn't say,

You wonder how it all went wrong within the
space of one day.

Too blind to realise that this had been happening
for a while,

And that it was about more than the fact that you
hadn't spoken in so long.

Constantly putting things ahead of her,

Someone that you should have held dear.

You can't see that you did anything wrong,

That it took her so long to see where you truly
belonged.

In your own mind that was on a throne,

But it became apparent to her that you actually
should have been alone.

Pride can create a hostile situation in the spaces
where love is supposed to provide vulnerability
and an intimate foundation.

Halting any progress to an otherwise loving
creation,

Through the sheer stubbornness and a lack of
attention, you gave to her.

Sloth

A tragedy of waiting,

Never making moves for yourself.

One of the worst types of self-sabotage,

Never going after what you want,

Trying to say that you're happy as you are.

Watching them fall in love with someone else
because you left it far too long.

And having to move on while constantly
thinking about what-if scenarios.

It's letting people you care about slip through
your fingers,

Because you're scared to hold on that bit tighter
for that bit longer.

You never feel like anything is actually yours,
everything you have you'd give up without the
fight you really want to give.

You fear commitment and what it means to people,

Never wanting to be responsible for someone else's happiness- only to miss out on your own.

Wrath

It's in the pulsing of your veins.

All consuming.

A fire spreading through your bones.

Clenching your fists.

Straining your eyes.

Born from mistakes only to make more.

A loss of control.

Seared into your mind.

Allowing for you to stew on it.

A volcanic eruption brewing.

Devastation following in its wake.

It's in losing yourself to the power you feel.

You feel bigger than you were.

But you're not the bigger person.

It's the shame of harming the person that you love without a rational mind.

It's throwing all caution to the wind.

Envy

It's the feeling that creeps up on you from the
way your stomach coils,

Twisting yourself into pieces so sharp you cut
yourself,

Working its way into your heart, clenching
painfully in your chest, and to the way your eyes
turn glacial when you see the way he looks at
her.

It's a poisonous substance that marks your
mouth in a bitter downturn of your lips when
you hear of their history.

Squinting your eyes, taking a new perspective of
your time together.

It's letting the comments get to you from his
group of friends, implying that he was happier
with her

A tease you used to be able to handle before you
let doubt affect how you two were together.

Greed

Never satisfied with what you have,

You grab and you take everything in reach.

You take everything a person can give,

Not caring when they have nothing left.

But when people take all they want,

Further down the line, they lose what they need.

Always taking for granted what you used to
have.

"You never know what you have until you lose
it" they say.

It's only a matter of time before you lose the
love of your partner.

Not The One You Want

If I'm not the one you want there

Then tell me at the door

Before my foot steps past the frame

If our relationship is not considered the same to you as it is by me

Then I'd rather know before I make myself at home

I don't need nor want a consolation

A hug, a chat, or any apologies

Before you shut me out

All I ask is that you please don't play any games

I'm past feeling the shame.

A Confession Gone Wrong

We were screaming and shouting,

And ripping apart at the seams.

When the space became too much,

The silence fell like the shattered pieces of our
dreams.

And I can't help remembering how we got here;

I confessed my love to you

and you acted like that wasn't fair.

I'd dared to tell you the truth

only for you to act like it was a burden to bear.

I don't understand why an 'I love you' was the
worst thing that you ever heard.

Hurt The One You Love

I would've hurt you.

Not on purpose, never intentional

But the matter of fact is that you hurt the people
you love and I loved you with everything I was

In all your innocence and naivety

Never believing that people were inherently bad

You had a light that warmed everyone you met

And I wasn't the only one whose darkness
wanted to snuff that out

I was weathered and beaten, acting like I weren't

And you had yet to see how the tables turned

For everybody basks in the light

And breaks in the dark

No Duty to Love

I don't want someone that I have to put my life
on hold for

Someone that I have to remember to talk to

Or remind myself that they're there

It shouldn't be a chore to have someone who is
there to care

But I need space for myself

And it's hardly a feeling that being with
someone else can replace

Is it too much to ask for someone to understand

That I'm not always myself when other people
are around.

Keep Coming back

And we both thought we knew the pain of letting
go

But the truth is between us we will never know

No matter how many times we try not to talk

We meet each other in the middle of a daily walk

We know each other too well

For this to be put to bed

We hurt and hurt each other

But there could truly be no other

That we could throw the ugliest parts of
ourselves at

And still be considered something beautiful to
look at.

There's a Heartbreak in Trying Again

Eyes catching despite the space between us,

We're both remembering the time it wasn't there.

Can't you see it in the shy smiles tinged with regret?

In the ways, we laugh at an old inside joke surrounded by old friends only to freeze and get caught in the memories of how much their laughs were adored.

It's in the way that you see them smile and wish with your whole heart that it was at you

It's in the way that your friends are getting tired of the awkwardness between you

So much so that they make plans for the group only to not turn up and leave you with each other.

It becomes a deep conversation that references old times,

And an offer for you both to share new times.

You had both made mistakes but you've grown
past that now, though it's clear that it will always
be held in your heart.

It's starting again as though you were never
apart.

Never Mine to Love

You were never mine to love,

But you're all I ever think about.

And if you ever find yourself thinking about
what we could've been,

Know that I spend my time hoping for such an
opportunity to come around.

You are my God,

And I'll pray for you every night.

Looking into the stars,

And hoping that they agree with my plight.